# Let's Travel in
# GREECE

Edited by Darlene Geis

A TRAVEL PRESS BOOK

PICTURE ACKNOWLEDGMENTS

The full-color illustrations in this book are the work of the following photographers and artists, whose collaboration is gratefully acknowledged. Photographed in Greece by Ace Williams (1, 2, 4, 6, 10, 12, 15, 17, 19, 21, 23, 24, 25, 28, 29); Orville Goldner (3, 5, 7, 8, 9, 11, 14, 16, 20, 22, 26, 31); Alfred Pirk (13, 27, 30); Sabine Weiss, from Rapho-Guillumette (18); Dandelet, from Shostal (32). For the black-and-white photographs we wish to thank Ace Williams; Orville Goldner; Davis Pratt from Rapho-Guillumette; Three Lions; Nellys; the Royal Greek Information Service, New York; Magnum; Black Star; and The Metropolitan Museum of Art, Purchase 1890, Levi Hale Willard Bequest. The map was made by Emerson Barron (Mann Associates), and the drawings by H. Lawrence Hoffman. Designed by Mann Associates.


New edition published 1964 by CHILDRENS PRESS, INC., Chicago.
Published simultaneously in Canada. Lithographed in the U.S.A.
Library of Congress Catalog Card Number: 64-20810

# CONTENTS

YUGOSLAVIA
BULG
ALBANIA
MACEDONIA
Salonica
Mt. Olympus
EPIRUS
Meteora
Trikkala
Pindus Mts.
THESSALY
IONIAN SEA
Mesolóngion
Delphi
ATTICA
Gulf of Corinth
Daphni
Corinth Canal
Athens
Salamis
PELOPONNESUS
Epidaurus
Mycenae
Nauplia
Sparta
MEDITERRANEAN
1–8
9
10
11
12–13
14
15
16
17
18
19
20
21
22
23
24
25
26
27
28
29
30
31
32

# Locales of thirty-two full-color pictures

# GREECE, IMMORTAL LAND

WHEN you see it on a map, the little country of Greece stretches like a many-fingered hand down into the Mediterranean. And that is the hand, gnarled with mountains, that rocked the cradle of our civilization. So when you visit Greece, even for the first time, it is like coming home again to the place where many of the finest ideas of beauty, of government, of philosophy were born. The Greeks had a word for most of these ideas—*democracy, algebra, geometry, architecture, ethics, drama, poetry, politics, athletics*—and many nations have taken over their words as well as the ideas.

This little hand, flinging its scattered islands into the seas surrounding it, cast its ideas even farther. They have taken root in every country of the Western world. Yet the whole of modern Greece, including the islands, is somewhat smaller than the state of Illinois. A little more than 50,000 square miles is the total area, and much of that is hilly, rocky, barren land unfit for cultivation. The Greek peasant cultivates his few poor acres with patience and perseverance. If he can have a vineyard, some olive trees and a patch of pasture for his donkey and sheep, he considers himself lucky. After all, he will tell you, when the world was created, God sifted the earth through a giant sieve. He tossed some good soil here, and some good soil there, but He threw the stones over His shoulder. And the place where the stones landed, the peasant explains with a shrug of resignation, was Greece.

But though her land is poor, Greece is generously endowed with coast line. See on the map how the land is wedded to water in hundreds of coves and inlets, bays and gulfs. With such an intermingling of sea and land it is not surprising that the ancient Greeks ranked Poseidon (*poh*-SIGH-*dun*), god of the sea, as one of their most important deities.

No town in Greece is more than seventy-five miles from the water, and so it is natural that many Greek men take to the sea for a living. Much of Greece's income today, as in olden times, comes from her shipping. As we travel in Greece, we too will be aware of the sea around us. That and the mountains, visible nearly every place we go, are the most vivid first impressions of the country.

For a land so small in area, Greece displays great contrasts and variety within its borders. That is why, if you visit only one section of Greece or see it during only one season, you will find it hard to recognize the country in other pictures. Greece can be both brown and green, barren and lush, subtropical and alpine. If we start in the north and work our way down the Greek peninsula, we run the whole gamut of climate and topography.

## MACEDONIA, COUNTRY WITHIN A COUNTRY

The principal northern province is Macedonia (*mass-eh*-DOH-*nee-ah*), homeland of Alexander the Great, who carried Greek language and civilization to much of the world then known, including India. Macedonia stretches across the top of the Aegean (*ee*-JEE-*an*) Sea, hilly, green and wild. Tobacco is a big crop here; but more important still, Macedonia is the breadbasket for the hot, dry south. Most of the grain that feeds the rest of Greece grows in this cooler climate under cloudy Macedonian skies. The Byzantine and Turkish periods in Macedonia's troubled history have left their marks on the towns and people, giving them a character quite distinct from those in the south. Salonica (*sal-oh*-NEE-*kuh*), the busy seaport and chief city of Macedonia, seems to bear little kinship with Athens, for example. The classical perfection of ancient Greece is absent here, but the lavish and mysterious East has left its ornate stamp on the city.

## EPIRUS, HOME OF THE BRAVE

On the other side of the peninsula, bordering the Ionian Sea, is the mountainous province of Epirus (*ee*-PIE-*rus*). Harsh and rugged, the mountains and plateaus are the home of a tough and valiant people who shepherd their flocks on the remote uplands, as their ancestors have done for centuries. One tough old king of Epirus was Pyrrhus (PEER-*us*), who, in 279 B.C., won a costly victory over the Romans. Success at a terrible price has been called a "Pyrrhic victory" ever since he counted up his few surviving soldiers and said ruefully, "One more such victory over the Romans and we are utterly undone!"

*This sturdy peasant comes from the wild land to the north where men and mountains are roughhewn.*

The mountains of Epirus are as snowy as the Alps from early December until spring. Yet one small section of this rugged province has lemon and orange groves, and rice paddies that flourish during the warm spring and summer months.

## THESSALY, GARDEN OF THE GODS

To the east of Epirus, separated from it by the central spine of the Pindus Mountains, is the fertile plain of Thessaly. Here fat flocks graze, and orchards and vineyards and olive groves thrive. In one of these valleys is a strange sight. Masses of rock rise 85 to 300 feet into the air, like vast stalagmites. Twenty-three monasteries were built on top of these weird pinnacles centuries ago—accessible only by rope and nets worked by windlass from the top, or by almost vertical ladders—and seven of them are still actively functioning. They are called the Meteora (*mee-tee*-OR-*ah*), or "those that hang in the air."

Religion has always played an important part in Greek life. The Emperor Constantine established Christianity as the official religion in this area more than 1,600 years ago. Today the national religion is that of the Orthodox Church. It is governed by a synod, or council, of Greek bishops, at whose head is the Archbishop of Athens. The higher clergy and the monks who live in the monasteries are not permitted to marry. But the parish priests, or *papas,* may marry, and many of them do.

From earliest times the Greeks peopled their country with contradictory, whimsical, powerful and charmingly human deities. Mt. Olympus, in the north of Thessaly, was the penthouse headquarters for this divine group. Nearby are Mt. Pelion and Mt. Ossa; according to legend, they were piled upon each other by the jealous Titans, early giant deities, in their effort to get at the Olympian gods and rule in their place. But the lawless giants were defeated and sent to the dark underworld, and the gods continued to rule from Olympus.

## CENTRAL GREECE, THE HEART OF THE COUNTRY

Centuries before the Christian era, when the Olympian gods still watched over Greece, Attica—Athens and its environs—was the core of Greek civilization. Today the modern bustling capital of Athens and its nearby seaport, Piraeus (*pie*-REE-*us*), are again the heart of Greece. "Greece within Greece," they say proudly of Athens. And for most travelers it is the Attic landscape, with its clear light, its classic ruins, its green mountains and distant sea, that really spells Greece.

The intermingling of past and present, evident everywhere in Greece, is most dramatic in Athens. Here is the twentieth-century boom town, with its slick new apartment buildings, its streetcars and automobiles, its neon signs; and rising above it, the hill of the Acropolis (*uh*-KROP-*oh-lis*), crowned with pillared ruins.

*The Olympic Games originated in ancient Greece with the ancestors of these young ballplayers.*

The Parliament, the Palace and the University are in Athens today, and the city is once again the seat of government and learning, though it has been the capital of modern Greece for only about 125 years. Greece won her independence from Turkey as recently as that. Now she is a constitutional monarchy, with an elected parliament, a prime minister, a cabinet and a king. The present King of the Hellenes is Constantine, who succeeded his father, the late King Paul I, in 1964.

Of all the famous cities of ancient Greece, Athens is the only one that is "alive" today. Delphi (DEL-*figh*), Sparta, Olympia, Corinth are now only ruins or archaeological diggings, with a few small peasant settlements nearby. During the Turkish rule, Athens too had faded from her former greatness, and was just a scraggly market town until the Greeks won their independence. Today, the Athenians have not only built a modern city; they have also painstakingly restored the ruins, so long neglected, of their past greatness.

For the Greeks are a proud and patriotic people. Their pride and patriotism embrace not only their modern state, but their ancient heritage as well. The poet Shelley described them with these two lines:

*Her citizens, imperial spirits,*
*Rule the present from the past.*

Certainly no modern Greek is unaware that his country gave the world great philosophers like Aristotle, Plato and Socrates; statesmen like Pericles (PEHR-*ih-kleez*); Herodotus (*heh*-ROD-*oh-tus*), father of history; Hippocrates (*hih*-POCK-*ruh-teez*), father of medicine; Euclid (YOU-*klid*), the mathematician. The modern Greek, so proud of his ancestry, often gives these illustrious names to his children.

## THE PELOPONNESUS, LAND OF MYTHS

To the south and west of Athens, and separated from the mainland of Greece by a fairly recent canal, is the Peloponnesus (*pel-oh-puh*-NEE-*sus*). This land of mountains and fertile plains has a history rooted in the oldest Greek myths. It was named after Pelops, son of King Tantalus and brother of weeping Niobe (NIGH-*oh-be*). Tantalus killed Pelops, his own son, and served him up as the main course in a banquet for the gods. With this tricky *pièce de résistance* he hoped to find out if the gods really knew everything. Of course, the gods *were* omniscient; they realized what Tantalus had done, and so they brought Pelops back to life and punished his sinful father in a way that has been known ever since as tantalizing. He was placed in a lake, with water up to his lips and tempting fruit nearby. But whenever he reached for food or drink, they retreated.

Corinth; Olympia, where the Panhellenic Games were held; Mycenae (*my*-SEE-*nee*), kingdom of Agamemnon; Sparta, the earliest totalitarian state—all of them, with their fascinating stories and accomplishments, are now stony ruins scattered over the Peloponnesus. Today this land, steeped in the blood of Greece's tragic history, is fertile with crops of mulberry, grapes, figs, olives, dates, oranges and currants, which take their name from Corinth. The sturdy peasants who inhabit the land seem to be a far cry from their terrible ancestors of the dark deeds. Watching their bands of musicians as they gaily make the rounds of all the local summer feasts, it is hard to realize that the heroes and heroines of Greek tragedy, and the Spartan boy with the fox under his shirt, are in the bloodlines of such a merry people.

But, by and large, the modern Greeks are probably much like their forerunners of classic times. Like them, they are a mixture of many strains. For Greece has always been prey to invading strangers who beached their boats on her shores, or marched down from the lands to the north, and stayed to populate the land. She has been conquered and overrun by Visigoths, Romans, Slavs, Frankish Crusaders and Turks, who have intermingled with the original early tribes. The modern Greek is usually dark, flashing-eyed, and short but well-built. His language is still recognizable as the Greek spoken over two thousand years ago.

Like his ancestors, the modern Greek is quick-witted, original, animated, with a lively imagination and a delight in discussion. He still talks politics and has a fierce love of freedom, which he has finally achieved; at last he is master in his own country. Above all, the modern Greek is warm and hospitable. No one can long feel himself a stranger in Greece. The citizens of this small country open their doors wide in welcome, and happily share with us their modest resources as well as the glories of their past.

*Athens today is a bright new city spreading at the foot of verdant Mt. Lycabettus.*

# let's travel in

# GREECE

# AN EVZONE: ELITE ROYAL GUARDSMAN

THIS Evzone (EHV-*zohn*) guard standing at attention is a symbol of the modern Greek nation. He is a member of the elite King's Guard Battalion, the cream of the Greek army, whose record in the last war was a brilliant one. Dressed in khaki kilts and wool stockings, the Evzones drove back Mussolini's soldiers even though enemy planes dominated the skies over Athens.

The short-skirted blue and red uniform is an adaptation of the Greek national costume. On holidays, for parades and official ceremonies the Evzones wear the national costume—forty yards of pleated white linen *fustanella,* or kilt, ten yards of billowing sleeve, and a snug, black jacket embroidered in silver and blue. The outfit may look like a ballet dancer's, but it originated with tough Greek mountaineers long ago. Like the Scottish highlanders, they found a kilt the most practical costume when leaping from crag to crag in their wild upland country.

*Skirted Evzones stride briskly on parade, forming a dashing pattern as they pass.*

In peacetime the most important function of the Evzones is to guard the king. Here we see one of them standing at attention near his sentry box in front of the great white Royal Palace. Every Sunday a platoon of these guards, wearing their crisp, white dress uniforms, marches through Constitution Square to the Tomb of the Unknown Soldier for an impressive changing of the guard. Athenians love a parade, and they crowd the square on Sundays to watch these colorful soldiers march past.

# CONSTITUTION SQUARE: CENTER OF ATHENIAN LIFE

HERE is Constitution Square on an ordinary day. It is almost always crowded—with Athenians and visitors alike, who find that its hundreds of small chairs give them a front-row seat at the spectacle of the town's busy life. Fashionable hotels, cafés and pastry shops are grouped around the square, but the most notable building is the old Royal Palace, which is now the House of Parliament. It was from the Palace balcony in 1843 that the Greek Constitution was proclaimed to the exuberant people in the square below.

The Athenians are no less exuberant today, and the café talk in the square is still, to a large extent, political. After work the Athenians drift toward the square for coffee and sticky-sweet pastries, a taste carried over from the days of Turkish domination. But those with lean purses may order a plain glass of water for a small tip. Fortunately, in Athens as elsewhere, talk is cheap and the conversation goes on long after darkness has fallen, when the square sparkles with lights. Greek democracy was born 2,400 years ago, and the modern Greeks still have that passionate interest in politics that distinguished their ancestors and led them to invent a new form of government in which every citizen could have his say.

The glorious past is very much present in Greece today. Beyond this square—the center of modern Athenian life—rises the hill of the Acropolis, symbol of Athens' past greatness. At night the pale columns of the Parthenon (PAR-*theh-non*) are illuminated on the hilltop, and the classic building gleams like a bright beacon above the city.

# THE ACROPOLIS: RUIN-CROWNED HILL

THE Acropolis is still the high heart of modern Athens, even as it was in ancient times. We see it in this picture, radiant in the sunlight, and marvel that this little hill had such a far-reaching influence on Western civilization. The Acropolis was fortified by the tribes who lived here long before recorded history. Traces of the old walls that they built still remain within the newer ones. Today the rocky fortification is topped with marble ruins, and the Acropolis floats above the city like a serene and ageless island, belonging to the present and to eternity.

In the early days the Athenians used the Acropolis as a place to worship their patron goddess, Athena (*uh*-THEE-*nuh*). But in the fifth century B.C., the conquering Persian army stormed the fortifications, burned the temples, and smashed the sacred statues, leaving the Acropolis a blackened monument to war. The Athenians finally vanquished the Persians at the nearby Bay of Salamis (SAL-*uh-miss*) in 480 B.C. After that great naval victory Athens entered her golden age. The Athenians returned to their ravaged Acropolis, and under the leadership of Pericles determined to crown it with lasting monuments to victory and to the goddess who had helped them achieve it.

*Busy Venizelos Street shows us modern Athens with all the trappings of twentieth-century civilization.*

# THE PROPYLAEA: ENTRANCE TO THE SACRED HILLTOP

THE winding way that leads to the Acropolis is followed today by worshipers of beauty who come from distant parts of the world to marvel at these antique splendors. In Athens' glorious heyday this was the path followed by the great Panathenaic (*pan-ath-eh-*NAY-*ick*) Procession. Every four years there was a great celebration in honor of Athena; it lasted several days, and its climax was the bringing of the new peplos (PEP-*lus*), or robe, to the statue of the goddess.

The procession moved along the Sacred Way winding from Athens up to the Propylaea (*prop-ih-*LEE-*uh*), or monumental entrance, which you can see at the extreme left. It was designed as an imposing portal to the Parthenon. Between its columns passed the long line of maidens and young men, the Athenian cavalry, and garlanded bulls, sheep and goats intended for sacrifice. We know exactly how the procession must have looked, because the sculptor Phidias (FID-*ih-us*) captured it in the marble carvings that encircle the Parthenon. A large section of this frieze, known as the Elgin marbles, is in the British Museum in London. But part of it still adorns the broken temple, and the marble people and animals seem to breathe with life after all these centuries.

The chaste and elegant little temple at the right of the Propylaea is the Temple of Athena Nike (NY-*kee*), Goddess of Victory. Usually Victory has been represented with wings, but here, legend says, the Athenians had chopped hers off so that she could never fly away from their city, and Athens would be victorious forever.

# THE PARTHENON: RELIC OF A GOLDEN AGE

HERE is the Parthenon. Probably no building in history has been so universally acclaimed for its perfection. Pericles ordered the Parthenon to be built of the fine-grained white marble cut out of Mt. Pentelikon (*pen*-TEL-*ih-kahn*), not far to the northeast of Athens. In Pericles' day the decorations above the columns and the background for the marble carvings were painted red and blue with gilt accents. Time has erased the bright colors and weathered the marble to the luminous golden glow that we see now.

Measurements help to explain why the "simple" pillared rectangle of the Parthenon is so pleasing to the eye. The architects built without using straight lines! They knew a thing or two about optical illusions, so they arched all the horizontals a little, and inclined the vertical pillars toward the inside of the temple, with the result that we have the illusion of straightness without the deadly stiffness that straight lines would have given. The Doric columns themselves taper a little toward their sturdy capitals, but what makes them so satisfying to the eye is the gently swelling curve of the vertical line. This eye-pleasing trick is called entasis (EN-*tah-sis*) and has been used by architects up to the present, as have the mathematically formulated proportions that give the old Greek temples their harmony of form.

*The ruins of the Parthenon are a haunting echo of this stately perfection. The model shows the temple in its unscarred youth.*

# THE AGORA: MARKET SQUARE OF ANTIQUITY

AT THE foot of the Acropolis this field of rubble lies, all that is left to us of the old Agora (AG-*oh-rah*). The Agora was the principal square of ancient Athens and the center of its public life. It was the Main Street, village green and city hall of antiquity, contained in six crowded acres. The ruins and foundations of the stately Agora buildings—the Senate, the Archives, many temples, shops, and the Gymnasium—all have been uncovered by archaeologists working here for the past hundred years. Much of the recent excavating has been done by the American School of Classical Studies, with money from John D. Rockefeller, Jr., and through a grant from the Marshall Plan.

Facing us is a reconstruction of the Stoa of Attalus (AT-*uh-luhs*). Its long portico once housed a row of shops, but now the Agora Museum exhibits its treasures here. Mt. Lycabettus (*lick-ah-*BET-*us*) and the buildings of modern Athens rise in the background. Look across this little patch of ground and try to imagine the Agora when all of its proud edifices stood white and immaculate in the clear Athenian sunlight. In those days philosophers walked here, conversing with their followers—Socrates (SOCK-*rah-teez*), Diogenes (*die-*AHJ-*eh-neez*), and the Stoic Zeno (ZEE-*no*) were well-known in the Agora. Zeno's philosophy was named Stoicism because he taught in one of the pillared buildings called a stoa. And St. Paul the Apostle mingled with the crowds in this very place 1,900 years ago where he "disputed in the market daily with them that met with him."

The Agora was the scene of political meetings, too. This is where the Assembly voted, and one of their practices was to vote for the banishment of any individual who threatened to become too powerful in the state. The ballots were fragments of pottery called ostracons (oss-*truh-kons*)—from which we get our word ostracism—and thousands of these fragments have been found here, inscribed with the names of persons to be banished from Athens.

# ARCHAEOLOGIST AT WORK: RECONSTRUCTING THE PAST

THE glory that was Greece is scattered in millions of fragments that must be painstakingly assembled, like the pieces of a jigsaw puzzle. Then the picture emerges of a civilization long past, whose achievements have scarcely been matched by any other people. Here we see an archaeologist putting together bits of broken pottery that were dug up in the Agora. The fragments have scientific as well as artistic value. Different types of pottery help to date the civilizations they came from, and words or drawings tell about the lives of the people who made them. And of course the vases that can be pieced together are precious works of art.

The site of the Agora was known for a long time, but it was covered with buildings until 1931. Then the district was set aside by law as an archaeological zone, the newer buildings were demolished, and large-scale excavations brought to light the ground plan and remains of the ancient market place. In sheds and workrooms like the one in this picture, dedicated scientists are busy reconstructing the civic center of ancient Athens. Fortunately Greece was always rich in durable building materials, and many of the old columns and their capitals still remain. Eventually they will be set in place again, and throngs of modern Athenians can gather where their forefathers did in the Agora's public park.

*The face of classic Greece stares with marble gaze from the Stoa of Attalus.*

# ACADEMY OF SCIENCE: MODERN GREEK BUILDING

FEW examples of ancient Greek temples are still intact, but there are any number of modern buildings that have borrowed the classic style, and from them we can form some idea of how the old buildings looked in their prime.

Since almost all Western countries went overboard for public buildings in the Greek style, it is only to be expected that Athens, especially, should have many modern examples of Doric and Ionic *(eye-*ON*-ik)*. After all, they are her rightful heritage.

Here is the Academy, built about seventy-five years ago of the very best Pentelic marble—just like the Parthenon. The architect studiously worked in the ancient style, using slender, fluted Ionic columns with scrolls at the top, pediments decorated with statues, and touches of color and gilding. It is true that the old buildings had the vitality of an original, while the Academy seems cold and mechanical. Still, it gives us some idea of what we might have seen more than two thousand years ago in ancient Athens when Greek genius flourished here.

*Greek temples were built in three main styles: Doric, at left; Ionic, in center; and Corinthian, at right.*

Today the learned men in the arts and sciences meet in the Academy. And nearby Athens University is built in the same architectural style. Both physically and intellectually, ancient Greece has been revived in Athens.

# MOUNT PENTELIKON: ANCIENT MARBLE QUARRY

THE enduring beauty of Athens' pillared temples has its source here in the fine white marble of Mt. Pentelikon. The ancient Greeks, finding that the mountain's dazzling stone was perfectly suited to their architecture, began to quarry here as long ago as 570 B.C. Marble from other sources was used for sculpture and trimming, but the Pentelic marble graced the noblest buildings of the classical age, as it does many of their modern counterparts.

Though Pentelikon is eleven miles from Athens, the Greeks ingeniously transported the marble slabs to their city. We can still see the markings of their old quarries and can tell from them what the procedure must have been. The Greeks sawed long blocks of marble, freeing them from the surrounding stone with wooden wedges, moistened so that they would swell. They cut the marble roughly into the required shapes right on the spot, and moved the slabs down the mountainside on wooden sledges that ran along a paved track.

As you can see in this picture, the newly quarried marble is snow-white. When it has been exposed to the atmosphere for a time, the iron in the stone oxidizes and gives Pentelic marble its tawny, golden hue. A tiny lichen thrives on this stone, and in the course of time it transforms the smooth white surface to a warm, powdery iridescence. Age and the peculiar characteristics of Pentelic marble have combined to enhance the artistry of the early Greek builders.

Athens is ringed by mountains, and they have given its citizens more than scenic beauty. Mt. Hymettus (*high*-MET-*us*) was famous for scented honey as well as for marble, and the mountain springs of each peak are renowned for their special waters. The mountains shelter and protect the city, yet they leave it open to the sea and its port of Piraeus to the west.

# HARBOR AT PIRAEUS: PORT OF ATHENS

HAD the city of Athens been landlocked, it probably never would have achieved prominence either in ancient times or now. Fortunately the site of Piraeus existed just five miles from Athens, and in the fifth century B.C. the great Athenian general Themistocles (*thee*-MISS-*toe-kleez*) built a seaport there and ensured Athens' access to it by means of a connecting fortification called the Long Walls.

The busy waterfront today is crowded not only with caiques (*kah*-EEKS), the sailing craft that ply between the mainland and its scattered islands, but with coastal steamships and foreign ships for which Piraeus is a port of call. It does not take much imagination to see, in place of these modern craft, the stately triremes (TRY-*reems*) of antiquity. It was here that these war galleys with their three tiers of oars gathered on the eve of great naval expeditions, and here that the ceremony was performed awarding crowns to the first three captains to report for duty.

*A fisherman serenely mends his net amid the hubbub and confusion of the bustling waterfront.*

Today the maritime importance of Greece is commercial rather than military. Piraeus, with a population of half a million people, is the second largest city and the chief industrial center of Greece. There are over a hundred factories, mills, distilleries and metalworks here, as well as silos and storehouses for the vast amounts of cargo unloaded at the port.

ΑΓΙΑ
ΒΑΡΒΑΡΑ
ΚΥΘΝΟΥ

# ISLAND OF SALAMIS: BOATBUILDING TRADITION

NOT far from Piraeus is the historic island of Salamis, where this boatbuilder is at work. Behind him is the narrow waterway between Salamis and the mainland, where the Greeks won their great victory over the Persians in 480 B.C.

Nearly 2,500 years ago, when the Persians swept down on Athens, most of the Athenians escaped to the offshore island of Salamis and took a stand there against the Persians. Possibly this man is descended from one of those brave people who withstood the invader and changed the course of the civilized world. The Greek navy was smaller than the Persian fleet, and could have an advantage only if the superior enemy force engaged it in these narrow waters. By a clever ruse the Greeks got the Persians to do just that. While the Persian king Xerxes (ZERK-*seez*) watched from his hilltop throne overlooking the harbor, his great ships went down to disaster in the water below.

Some of the Persian ships had as many as two hundred oarsmen. It was impossible for them to maneuver in the crowded channel, and the smaller Greek vessels darted in, ramming the great hulls, setting fire to many of the wooden ships and dispersing the rest, which fled to safety. Xerxes' army was cut off from supplies, and he returned to Persia, never again to attempt the conquest of these hardy people.

The great age of Greece's commercial, political, and cultural supremacy began then, and she ruled the Mediterranean for many years. The wooden boat being built here is probably not very different from those long-ago vessels whose victory saved Greece. You can see that the beams are hand-hewn, and it is not hard to picture this scene taking place more than two thousand years ago.

# CHURCH AT DAPHNI: EARLY BYZANTINE GEM

TRAVELERS to Greece are usually so impressed by her classic antiquities that they overlook her second great legacy of art—the Byzantine. When in 323 A.D. the Emperor Constantine moved his capital from Rome to Byzantium—renamed Constantinople in 330 A.D.—the Byzantine Empire began, and Greece was a part of it. Under the new influence, Greece acquired her fair share of churches and art in the Byzantine style. One of the loveliest is the church and monastery at Daphni (DAF-*nee*), which we see here.

Old Greek temples were rectangular, and the first Greek churches followed this pattern. But the dome, which originated in the East, had great symbolic significance for the Byzantine church architects. It represented the celestial vault to them and made a perfect covering for a building constructed in the form of a cross. Where the lines of the cross intersected, the dome of heaven was placed, and you will see that most Byzantine churches follow this pattern, as does the church at Daphni. If we take the ancient Sacred Way out of Athens to the old city of mystery, Eleusis (*ee*-LOO-*sis*), we will pass Daphni on the way. The church was built on the site of a far older temple to Apollo, among the laurel groves sacred to the sun god. One of the marble columns of the pagan temple was imbedded in a wall here, and even now the sun seems to touch this quiet courtyard with special radiance.

*They also serve who only peel the onions. This monk knows there are many paths to heaven.*

# MONASTERY PAINTINGS: GREECE'S SECOND GREAT ART

THE sun-warmed stone exterior of a Byzantine church gives no hint of the splendor inside, where both color and design are brilliant and lavish. In the early days of Christianity, when people generally could not read, their churches had to be like gorgeous picture books illustrating the stories and ideals of their religion. Frescoes—or, in the case of richer churches, mosaics—covered every inch of space.

The pagan Greeks had extolled the human body in their art, picturing their deities as men and women. Then, in the fourth century, the Emperor Constantine issued an edict designed to stamp out paganism (it was he who devised the fig leaf to clothe the classical statues of antiquity). Naturalism in painting and sculpture was replaced with a flat, stylized rendering of garments and faces in an age that emphasized the spirit rather than the flesh. Painters now had to work according to rigid church rules. That is one reason why, from church to church, the similarity of Byzantine paintings is so striking. Only the artist's skill gave one church a masterpiece and another a mere decoration.

Even the arrangement of pictures in a Byzantine church follows a set pattern. The dome is reserved for the main figure of Christos Pantocrator (KRISS-*toss pan*-TOCK-*rah-ter*), Christ the All-Powerful Ruler, ringed by angels and prophets, always in prescribed poses. The walls, as we see them in this picture, could be painted only with stories of Christian feasts and full-length portraits of saints. The stiff and formal elegance of the draped figures is offset by bright colors and, in some cases, by the richness of gold and glittering gems set into the walls. The interior glows with light entering through numerous arched windows, as in all Byzantine churches, which were designed to unite worshipers inside a holy building. The pagan practice of worshiping in front of a temple under the naked sky had been abandoned, and with it passed the pillared rectangle designed as a backdrop for open-air ceremonials.

# BAY OF SALAMIS: EARLY MORNING HAUL

AFTER leaving Daphni and its wooded hills, we follow a wide road down to the sea. The misty blue water of the Bay of Salamis is a refreshing contrast to the parched and stony countryside. But however dry the Greek land is, it is never far from water. The sea makes up in its bounty for the miserly land that yields such meager crops. The fishermen cast their broad nets and are sure of a good haul, just as they were in the days when Poseidon ruled the sea.

Long ago this part of Greece was a sacred place to which pilgrims journeyed from Athens. The Sacred Way, which still exists as the main road from Athens to the rest of Greece, led to the city of Eleusis, famed for its Mysteries. The Mysteries were based on the old myth of Demeter (*deh-*MEE*-ter*), goddess of the harvest, whose temples and shrines were built at Eleusis. Only the initiated were permitted to enter the temple and take part in the rites, and they were considered then to be assured of a blissful afterlife in the Elysian Fields.

*Demeter, goddess of harvest, welcomes her lost daughter. The mystery of new life is celebrated in this myth.*

In this picture you can sense the ancient mystery still lingering in the very landscape. Mountains and distant water seem unreal and magical in the golden haze. The town of Eleusis, however, is a very prosaic place today. It is dedicated to the manufacture of soap, cement and spirits (alcoholic rather than ghostly). And smokestacks rise where once the proud columns of Demeter stood.

# CORINTH CANAL: MARITIME SHORT CUT

THE Bay of Salamis and the Gulf of Corinth are separated by a slender neck of land that joins the Peloponnesus to the rest of Greece. More than two thousand years ago the Greeks thought of cutting a canal across the Isthmus of Corinth, realizing that it would save their ships a two-hundred-mile voyage around the Peloponnesus. Off and on through the centuries Greek and Roman engineers made plans for the project.

Finally, in 67 A.D., the Roman emperor Nero actually began the digging. He used a golden shovel to start the work, and imported a slave labor force of six thousand prisoners from Judea who continued the excavation with less remarkable implements. But the canal was not completed. Instead, sailors still had to put their ships on rollers and move them clumsily overland on tracks as Augustus had done when he pursued the navy of Antony and Cleopatra.

The canal as you see it here was begun by a French company in 1882 and completed by a Greek firm eleven years later. When the engineers first began to cut the canal, they found the old Roman borings almost exactly on a line with their proposed route. This part of the country is barren and desolate, whipped by violent winds that prevent the growth of much vegetation. It is the legendary home of Sciron, a brigand who preyed on travelers and hurled them into the sea until the hero Theseus (THEE-*syoos*) put an end to him. The Peloponnesus has a longer history than the rest of mainland Greece, and the names from the distant past still exist here. But Sparta, Olympia, Mycenae amount to very little except for the ruins of their ancient glory. And even Corinth, once a flourishing and wealthy city, is now an unimportant town dozing on the rocky coast. The canal destroyed its position at the crossroads of the vital overland trade routes, and today St. Paul would no longer find it necessary to preach to the Corinthians about the evils of frivolity and luxury.

# WATERFRONT VILLAGE: GREEK WHISTLE STOP

ALONG the Gulf of Corinth little villages hug the shore, while the land rises behind them steep and hilly. The railroad, too, seeking level ground, has had to stay close to the water. In this picture we see one of these coastal towns with a small Greek train chugging past the very doorsteps. For all he cares at this moment, the young fisherman could have hooked a whale. Boys are the same all over the world when it comes to watching old 711 steam by; everything else is forgotten.

The row of kitchen chairs set up outdoors is typical of Greece. You will see them wherever people live—in certain sections of Athens and in the tiniest mountain hamlets. The homemade chair with its woven reed seat takes the place of a club membership. In this mild climate men sit outdoors to talk, read their papers, play cards or just watch the boats and trains go by.

In the early evening, especially, you will find them clustered around wooden tables on the sidewalks and playing a favorite game called tricktrack, an ancient form of backgammon that has been played in this part of the world for hundreds of years. The men will be drinking glasses of clear spring water, the favorite beverage of the Greek people. They are such connoisseurs that, like a Frenchman with wine, they can tell you what region or even what spring produced the water they are drinking. This water cult has existed since the days when early Greeks deified their fountains and attributed sacred properties to some of them.

The vista of mountains and sea is unchanged since Homer's times, and the inhabitants of the country today still delight in being out of doors where they can admire the tranquil grandeur of their land.

# QUAY AT NAUPLIA: AGE-OLD SEAPORT

THE city of Nauplia (NAW-*plih-uh*) is terraced on the slope of a rocky peninsula overlooking a blue gulf. Across the water the mountains of the Peloponnesus are shadowed in muted colors, forming a theatrical backdrop for the Bourdzi (BOORD-*zee*) Islet. Nauplia was a port of call more than 2,600 years ago for navigators who came from the lands to the east. Legend says that its founder was Palamedes (*pal-ah-*ME*-deez*), inventor of the nautical arts, lighthouses, the alphabet, and games of dice and backgammon—in short, the foreign culture received from abroad by early Greeks.

The Byzantines, Franks, Venetians and Turks all held this valuable naval station at one time or another. When the Greeks revolted against the Turks in 1821, they regained Nauplia, and from 1829 to 1834 it was the seat of the new Greek government. Today it is headquarters for many tourists who wish to visit nearby Mycenae and Epidaurus (*ep-ih-*DAW-*rus*).

One of the most unusual hotels in Greece is on the little island that looks like a floating fort. Bourdzi was originally a fifteenth-century Venetian fort, and later, because of its isolated position, it was used as a home for retired executioners. The Greek people had a superstitious dislike of executioners, and banned them from the community once their professional days were over. Its grim past forgotten now, Bourdzi is a pleasant retreat instead of a place of exile.

*Convivial Greeks gather for games and conversation—two favorite outdoor sports.*

# THE LION GATE: MYCENAE'S PRIMITIVE SPLENDOR

STANDING before the Lion Gate at Mycenae, we are on the very threshold of the legendary past. This city had its origin in the misty beginnings of the Bronze Age, some five or six thousand years ago, and its history intermingles with the great and bloody legends of ancient Greece. Homer, in the *Odyssey* and the *Iliad*, gave many clues about this region. In the past century the German archaeologist Schliemann (SHLEE-*mahn*), using Homer as a guide, began to dig here. He came upon the fabulous remains of the walled city, and found graves heaped with golden treasure that may have belonged to Agamemnon, king of Mycenae and leader of the Greeks in their war against Troy.

The Acropolis of Mycenae is a rocky citadel rising above a fertile plain. Rugged and windswept, the lonely ruins and the empty graves open to the sky are disquieting reminders of the early people who lived here. The massive blocks of stone that form the walls of Mycenae and the Lion Gate were set in place during the fourteenth century B.C., when the city was at the height of its power. By 1000 B.C. Mycenae had been conquered by the Greek-speaking Dorians from the north who waged war with arms of iron. Greek civilization, as we know it from written history, was about to dawn. And one of its legends was to be that the Cyclopes (*sy*-KLOH-*peez*), one-eyed giants of enormous strength, had built these immense walls.

*On the stage at Epidaurus we see a modern performance of a play that was written 2,400 years ago.*

# THEATER AT EPIDAURUS: EARLY DRAMA

OF ALL the arts, ideas and treasures bequeathed to us by the ancient Greeks, none has given more pleasure than the drama. The very word is Greek, and it means "a thing done or performed." Our modern plays are as different from the early Greek performances as a Broadway theater is from the open-air amphitheaters of antiquity. Yet, when we look at this great shell carved into a mountainside at Epidaurus, we know that our theater sprang directly from this one.

The city of Epidaurus was famous by the fourth century B.C. as a shrine to Asclepius (*as*-KLEE-*pee-us*), the god of medicine. In those days it was a combination of the Mayo Clinic, Lourdes and the Salzburg Festival. People flocked here to be treated or cured miraculously, and this theater which seats 14,000 persons gives us some idea of the hordes who came here in quest of health.

The tiers of seats curve around a circular floor, or orchestra, that is typical of the first Greek theaters. It originated in the circular threshing floors which can be seen to this day in parts of rural Greece. Oxen or donkeys are driven around and around in a circle over the grain until it is threshed. Way back in pre-Greek times this hard-packed threshing circle became the floor for fertility rites and dances, from which the drama later developed. The name *orchestra* came from the Greek word for dancing.

The acoustics in this remarkable theater are so good that the actors on the circular floor need only speak in their natural voices and we can hear them from the top row. Every year at Epidaurus, the National Theater of Greece performs the great tragedies of Sophocles, Aeschylus (ES-*kih-lus*) and Euripedes (*you*-RIP-*ih-deez*), and the witty comedies of Aristophanes (*ar-iss*-TOFF-*uh-neez*). Their notable words have echoed down the centuries and sounded in all the countries of the Western world.

# GIRL SPINNING: THE DISTAFF SIDE

YOU might see a sight like this almost anywhere in the Greek countryside. The women of Greece have been spinning their own thread from wool or flax through all the centuries of Greek history—and in this same primitive fashion. The peasant woman is holding a homemade distaff. That cotton-candy fluff at the top of it is flax. As she twists and turns the spindle in her right hand, she spins a thread off the distaff and winds it around the spindle. Long before the spinning wheel was invented, women spun thread this way, and in certain sections of Greece they spin it so fine that it can be woven into veils that are almost transparent. Homespun cloth is a necessity in this unmechanized country, where nearly everything the people wear is made by hand.

Peasant women carry their spinning equipment around with them as casually as American women carry their knitting. You might see them sitting by the roadside or walking across a field, or even jogging along a dusty road on muleback. In their hands are the fluff-topped distaff and the busily twirling spindle, trademarks of the Greek countrywoman.

Except in two or three big cities, the people of Greece lead a primitive life, and a hard one. Everything they need—the food they eat, the water they drink, the clothes on their backs—must be earned with hard work. Yet if you look at their faces you will see a serenity that is rare in the more cosmopolitan centers of the world.

# WOMEN WEAVING: PROUD ACCOMPLISHMENT

MANY small villages in Greece have a local fame for the quality of the rugs, household linens, laces and embroideries made by their women. Usually the most attractive objects produced in the village are exhibited outdoors, where their lively colors brighten the drab, dusty towns. In this picture we see two women weaving on a crude loom in front of their cottage. Each household has become a homecraft industry, with all the daughters, aunts, grandmothers and cousins pitching in to help the mother. Some do the spinning with distaff and spindle, some dye the thread or wool, others help with the weaving and the loom. All can be proud of the finished product, knowing it is the creation of many able hands.

The homecraft industries have been given a big boost by the government in recent years. Throughout Greece and the islands there are numerous Royal Handicraft Schools, whose aim is to revive and encourage the old arts. Along with new designs in lace, embroidery and weaving, the ancient patterns have been studied and reproduced.

Several thousand years ago Homer addressed this line to a woman in the *Odyssey:* "Go to thy chamber and see to thine own tasks, the loom and the distaff." In twentieth-century Greece it still applies.

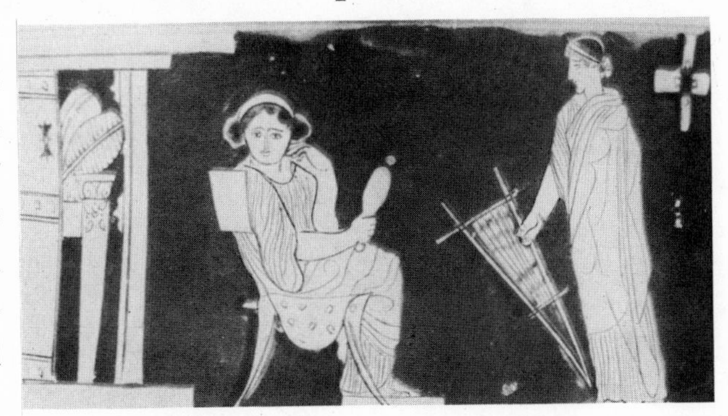

*One woman holds a mirror, the other an embroidery frame—the Eternal Feminine captured on an ancient vase.*

# RURAL VEHICLE: THE USEFUL DONKEY

EVERYWHERE in Greece you see the patient donkey. He is used for transportation. The country roads, where they exist at all, are rough and rocky paths winding up steep hills where only a sure-footed donkey can climb with ease. The ancient Greeks built their finest structures on hilltops, and consequently anyone who visits their ruins today must be prepared for an arduous uphill walk or a donkey ride.

The little beasts are also used for carrying firewood, sheaves of grain and household goods. They can refuel in any meadow or on a grassy hillside—an advantage they have over automobiles. Whenever villagers gather for church services or one of the many occasions for conviviality so dear to the Greek heart, the nearby fields are dotted with grazing donkeys—a picturesque version of a crowded parking lot. We see a typical rural street scene in this picture. The whitewashed stone houses, the muddy road, animals instead of automobiles, and the brightly painted cart with high latticed sides stamp this unmistakably as a Greek town. Country women seldom go bareheaded in the hot, glaring sun. Working in the fields they simply tie kerchiefs over their hair, but riding or walking, they remind us of the draped statues of classical times, with a dark veil covering their head and falling in graceful folds that might have been sculptured by an artist 2,500 years ago.

*Gypsy families wander along the roads of Greece—a carefree life for everyone but the donkeys.*

# FISHERMAN'S HUT: RUSTIC SPLENDOR

BEAUTY is ever-present in Greece, touching even the simplest scenes with glory. Here in the limpid light of early morning, a fisherman's hut is gilded by the rising sun, and water, sky and distant mountains seem to be painted by a master hand. It is no wonder that the Greeks used to worship nature and saw gods and goddesses in every field and forest, in the sun, the moon, the wind, the sea; and they saw them in tempest and earthquake as well as in the calm and gentle countryside. Although the land is poor, it rewards its inhabitants with views like this, and the Greeks have fought valiantly to keep it their own.

The fisherman's family in this placid picture lives in the town of Mesolóngion (*meh-so-*LONG-*gyon*), a historic place that was not always so peaceful. In 1825 Greek insurgents made a stand here against their Turkish oppressors. Greece had been a Turkish province for nearly four hundred years, and when the people finally revolted, they had the sympathy of many Europeans who had been nurtured on the culture of ancient Greece.

Lord Byron, the English poet, donated large sums of money to the cause of Greek independence, and he came to Mesolóngion himself in hopes of actually leading troops into battle. The fever-infested marshes that surround the town were his undoing, and Byron died here. Later France, England and Russia intervened on the side of the Greeks, though for less romantic reasons than Byron's. And in 1832 Greece became an independent kingdom, with a Bavarian prince as its ruler.

Mesolóngion is once again a quiet waterfront town with little to remind one of its heroic past—only modest monuments to Byron and to the victims of the siege grace a pretty tree-shaded square. But the eternal beauty of Greece endures here with no other monument than the land itself.

# COLUMNS AT DELPHI: HOME OF THE ORACLE

WE HAVE traveled east from Mesolóngion to Delphi, where the towering mountains split into a broad and steep ravine, a place of savage grandeur that has been sacred from the earliest times. This region has always been subject to earthquakes and terrible storms, and there have been numerous rocky landslides on the southern flank of Mt. Parnassus (*par*-NASS-*us*), where Delphi is perched. Steam and fumes issue from cracks in the rock. Here the awesome and terrifying majesty of Delphi existed in nature long before the fabled shrines were built in the seventh century B.C.

The Delphic Oracle was a woman, usually uneducated, who acted as a medium for the priests of Apollo. She sat on a tripod in a cave below the Temple of Apollo, breathing the intoxicating fumes that rose from a chasm in the rock. When she went into a trance, the priests took down her incoherent words and put them into cryptic verse. These pronouncements were usually open to broad interpretations, and consequently the Delphic Oracle was seldom proved wrong. The Oracle's fame lasted for more than a thousand years. She was consulted by foreign rulers, kings, would-be kings, and anyone else who could pay the fee for her counsel. The mountainside was terraced and thronged with buildings—a theater, a stadium, the Temple of Apollo, and treasury buildings of numerous cities and nations, filled with bounty for the gods. The Delphic Oracle was big business.

In this picture we are looking at the Tholos (THOH-*lohss*), a marble rotunda set on a terrace fringed with olive trees. This lovely circular building, like a garland of columns, is mysterious as well as beautiful. No one knows, to this day, what deity was honored by it. But Delphi itself was primarily sacred to Apollo. It was on a wall of his temple that the famous and difficult command was inscribed: "Know thyself." Not even the Delphic Oracle could impart that knowledge to her petitioners.

# PEASANT WOMEN: VIVID REGIONAL COSTUMES

THESE country women might be modern counterparts of the Delphic Oracle. The people of Greece share the timeless quality of their land, and their features are familiar to us from the carvings and paintings of long ago. The strong, smiling faces linger in our memory of the country, as striking a part of it as mountains, sea and brilliant sky.

Festivals have played an important part in Greek life from pagan times to the present, and in a country where everyday dress is dark and plain, the festive costumes reflect the richness of a long and varied history. The full skirts and tight bodices recall the wasp-waisted women of early Crete. Embroidered designs are often inspired by Byzantine church decorations, as is the heavy gold jewelry.

The women's costumes vary from one section of Greece to another, but whatever influences have shaped them, the dresses all have this in common: the material is fine and handsomely woven; the embroidery is a work of art. Greek women have excelled at these handicrafts since long before Penelope (*peh-*NEL-*oh-pee*), who wove patiently at her loom until Odysseus (*oh-*DISS-*use*) returned from the Trojan War. The Greek woman's costume is made to endure, for the people of this country feel that beauty should be imperishable.

*A chain of dancers moves in stately rhythm, re-creating the antique round dance of other times.*

# SHEPHERD AT TRIKKALA: FACE OF THE AGES

IN CENTRAL Greece, the plain of Thessaly spreads richly in contrast to the harsh mountains that tower above it. Greece is largely a barren land, and by comparison Thessaly is fruitful indeed. The mountain forests abound in game, and on the fertile lowlands farmers can raise cereals, tobacco and rice. But the farms are small, and there are not enough men to cultivate this land to its full potential.

The town of Trikkala (TRICK-*ah-lah*) lies almost at the center of Greece, and it is a busy market for the produce of Thessaly. In winter its population is swelled by the sturdy shepherds who bring their flocks down from the highland pastures to the north and west. We see one of them here, with a rugged bearded face that might have been described by Homer. He carries the traditional crook of olive wood called a *bastouni* (*bahs*-TOO-*nee*). Its wide wooden hook enables him to catch an errant sheep by the leg and pull it back to the flock. This is the original of the bishop's crosier, or pastoral staff, and its purpose is symbolically the same.

*These hard-working people know how to relax. A glass of wine, music, a shady tree, and the spirit is refreshed.*

Homer wrote of this ancient town, and it was famous, too, for a fine breed of horses whose spirited heads are preserved today in the marble carvings of the Parthenon. But visitors stay here now only because Trikkala is convenient to those marvels of Thessaly, the Meteora, which we are going to see next.

# THE METEORA: MONASTERIES IN THE AIR

THE plain of Thessaly was once the floor of a great inland sea. When the land shifted, the water drained out into the Aegean, leaving a dry basin ringed by hills and mountains. But the surging water carved out a forest of tall stone towers in one of the valleys—a kind of moon landscape. As we see here, the rocky towers rise straight up from the grassy slopes of this lonely valley. They are topped, not by eagles' nests, as one might expect, but by fourteenth-century monasteries known as Meteora, suspended between earth and heaven.

A group of Orthodox monks built these hermitages six hundred years ago so that they could withdraw from the tumult of their war-torn world. We can barely guess what patience and labor were required to erect twenty-three such buildings on these difficult peaks. Originally it was possible to reach the Meteora only by means of a net and rope, or a series of rickety ladders. Nowadays there are steps cut into the rock, but only seven of the monasteries are still inhabited. At the summit of each peak, within the monastery walls, there is, of all things, a garden. Great masses of brilliant flowers bloom up there, and blossoming fruit trees screen the distant view.

All the monks led rigorously austere lives, but one monastery carried things so far that their vow forbade any woman to approach or receive food even if she were dying of hunger. For about two hundred years the Meteora were rich and powerful; then they declined. The treasures in Byzantine art and illuminated manuscripts that the monks had stored up were sold or looted. Only a few paintings and crosses still remain. And, of course, the gardens.

# FARMHOUSE IN THESSALY: GRANARY OF GREECE

THESSALY and Macedonia, which is farther to the north, furnish Greece with most of her grain. But though these regions are known as the breadbasket for the rest of the land, they are not an overflowing basket of plenty. The amount of land suitable for cultivation in this arid and stony country of mountains has always been insufficient for its needs. Farms are small, and many of them are still plowed with primitive implements drawn by oxen or mules, although mechanized farm equipment is available for the larger co-operatives in the north.

The farmhouse in our picture is decked with the fruits of the field as though for Thanksgiving. Food was cherished in ancient times as a gift of the gods—Athena brought the olive tree, Dionysus (*die-oh-*NIGH-*sus*) the grapevine, and wildflowers for the honeybees blossomed in the footsteps of Aphrodite (*af-roh-*DIE-*tee*), goddess of beauty. Demeter was the goddess of harvest, and it was she who anchored people to the soil, taught them to eat bread and to enjoy the virtues of domesticity. Corn was her special crop, and the golden ears hanging from this house recall one of the most powerful beliefs of the pagan Greeks.

When Demeter's daughter was carried off to the underworld, the bereaved goddess refused to permit anything to grow in the earth until the girl was returned. The daughter was finally permitted to spend six months of the year with her mother. Then the earth blossomed and was fruitful, but for the six months of the daughter's absence in the nether world, corn and other growing things apparently died, only to achieve new life in the season of Demeter's reunion with her child. The ear of corn became a symbol of the mystery of continuing life, and those who were initiated into Demeter's cult achieved a tranquil sense of their own spiritual immortality. These two peasant women, elderly handmaidens of Demeter, seem to have some kinship with the initiates of times long past.

# SMALL BOY, LARGE LOAF: BREAD OF THE COUNTRY

YOU see children everywhere in Greece, with eyes as dark as ripe olives, and a vivacity and eagerness that are the heritage of their energetic forebears. The famine and misery of the war and postwar years are over, and pinch-faced youngsters suffering from malnutrition are no longer a heartbreaking fact of Greek life.

This plump little fellow is carrying an enormous loaf of bread. The Greek staff of life is delicious. Perhaps this is the result of a long tradition of giving beauty and goodness to even the homely necessities. In ancient times, Greek inspectors carefully judged the loaves for size and quality.

Sometimes the bread is baked in crusty wheels like the one this boy is holding. Very often the loaf is this size, but doughnut-shaped. Always the crust is brown and crisp, and the inside firm and white. In villages and hamlets off the beaten track the people eat a heavy but nutritious black bread, or a thick yellow loaf made of corn. Neither peasant nor plutocrat asks for anything better than a piece of bread dunked in a bowl of clabber (curdled goat's milk), a favorite Greek snack. And the gods on Olympus might well have used bread like this to mop up their nectar and ambrosia.

*This boy is earning his daily bread by helping to make raisins from luscious green grapes.*

# PASTORAL LANDSCAPE: TIMELESS SCENE

THE old gods seem to live again when we look at the flower-strewn countryside of Greece and remember the myths of Pan, god of flocks and pastures, and the nymphs and shepherds who used to sport in just such fields as these. The air is fragrant with lavender and thyme, and the piping of shepherds still echoes sweetly from hill to hill. Sheep and goats graze in the meadows as they did in those idyllic days when the world was young. Possibly the prevalence of nymphs was greatly exaggerated by the ancient story-tellers, but the men of the twentieth century who watch over flocks and live on milk and cheese are not very different from the shepherds of old except in the way they dress.

Sheep and goats are an important source of food, wool and leather. Since the country cannot support large herds of cattle, these smaller animals who can climb the rocky hills and forage on meager pickings must take their place. Goats have nibbled away at young trees and destroyed valuable farmlands, but although their grazing habits denude the land, the shepherds are loath to restrain them. The fields surrounding country villages are dotted with grazing flocks, and if you stop for a meal you will feast on eggs, on cheese and butter made from sheep or goat milk, on figs, melon or grapes, and on the ever-present olives of Greece. This was the simple fare of the happy denizens of Arcadia long ago, and these pastoral people today are a link with the peaceful past.

*The music of Pan is heard wherever the shepherd boy plays his haunting tune.*

ΠΕΙΡ. 297

# SHIP AT SALONICA: CITY OF THE NORTH

THIS Macedonian seaport, third largest city in Greece, has none of the afterglow of classical antiquity that we find in other sections of the country. The old parts of town are Byzantine and Turkish, but most of the city is bright and modern, newly built after a calamitous fire in 1917. Salonica's climate, like Macedonia's, is continental rather than Mediterranean—cooler, damper and conducive to richer vegetation. Even in ancient times the Greeks considered the Macedonians foreigners because they spoke a different language. Yet it was a Macedonian king, Alexander the Great, who conquered most of the known world in the fourth century B.C. and spread Hellenistic culture far beyond the confines of its tiny homeland.

Salonica, sometimes called Thessalonica, was named for a Macedonian queen who was the half-sister of Alexander. St. Paul founded a church here, his second in Europe, and his Epistles to the Thessalonians were addressed to the parishioners of this city. Ever since the Middle Ages, Salonica has been a vital seaport for landlocked Central Europe, serving as its link with the commerce of Asia. Situated on the Gulf of Salonica at the head of the Aegean Sea, its deep bay permits large ships to unload their cargo directly on the quay, as we see them doing in this picture. This is a far more economical procedure than the one followed at Piraeus, where cargoes from large ships must be transferred to freight barges before they can be put ashore. Salonica is competing hotly with her sister city to the south.

The white buildings overlooking the harbor have a view of the maritime commerce that will be an important factor in the economic future of Greece. But behind them the famous Byzantine churches of Salonica are its jeweled mementoes of a fabulous past.

# ETERNAL GREECE: SUNSET ON THE ACROPOLIS

As a last view, nothing can sum up the spirit of Greece better than this poetic sight of the Parthenon at sunset. Between the great pillars of the Propylaea an unforgettable picture of Greece is framed. There stands the Parthenon, broken yet majestic. Behind it in the dusky twilight lies the city of Athens, and disappearing into the background the mountains of Attica seem to roll endlessly toward the setting sun. The pillars themselves have a mellowness that can come only from the combination of fine material and great age. The nicks and bruises of time seem to have enhanced the original artisans' design, and it is hard to believe that these buildings were ever any more beautiful when the columns were white and sharply new.

We must remember that people come to Greece today not only as visitors to the modern country but as pilgrims to the past. This twentieth-century girl with her red skirt flaring between the ancient columns does not look out of place. There is a sense of vivid life in the past as well as the present.

Perhaps the timelessness of Greece and her fundamental contribution to Western culture were best described by Thucydides (*thoo*-SID-*ih*-*deez*), historian of her golden age, when he wrote:

*For we are lovers of the beautiful*
*Yet simple in our tastes,*
*And we cultivate the mind without loss of manliness.*

*The future of Greece is in her children, inheritors of a glorious past.*

## CHIEF GODS IN GREEK MYTHOLOGY

ZEUS (Roman name, Jupiter)—*Supreme deity, "father of gods and men." Lord of the sky, hurler of thunderbolts, giver of victory.*
HERA (Roman name, Juno)—*Wife and sister of Zeus. Goddess of marriage.*
POSEIDON (Roman name, Neptune)—*Brother of Zeus. Ruler of the sea, tamer of horses. A blow of his trident caused earthquakes and storms.*
HADES (Sometimes called Pluto)—*Brother of Zeus. God of the underworld, ruler of the dead, god of wealth, precious minerals and metals buried in the earth.*
ATHENA (Roman name, Minerva)—*Sprang fully armed from the head of Zeus, her father. Protectress of Athens, goddess of victory, health, wisdom, law and civic virtues.*
APOLLO—*Son of Zeus. God of manly youth and beauty, of poetry and music; a divinity of the sun.*
ARTEMIS (Roman name, Diana)—*Twin sister of Apollo. Virgin huntress, a divinity of the moon.*
APHRODITE (Roman name, Venus)—*Goddess of love and beauty, who arose from the foam of the sea.*
HEPHAESTUS (Roman name, Vulcan)—*Husband of Aphrodite. God of fire and metal-working arts, maker of armor and weapons.*
ARES (Roman name, Mars)—*Armored god of war, consort of Aphrodite, more popular with Romans than with Greeks.*
HERMES (Roman name, Mercury)—*Swift messenger of the gods; deity of roads and commerce, science, luck, cunning and thievery. Represented with winged sandals, hat and wand.*
HESTIA (Roman name, Vesta)—*Goddess of the hearth, guardian of the home. Her sacred flame was carried by Greeks to each new colony they founded.*

## SOME FAMOUS NAMES IN GREEK HISTORY

HOMER (c. 900 B.C.)—*Western literature originated with this blind poet's epic of Trojan War*—The Iliad—*and of Ulysses' long journey home*—The Odyssey.
SAPPHO (c. 600 B.C.)—*She was greatest of early Greek lyric poets.*
PERICLES (c. 490-429 B.C.)—*Statesman under whose thirty-two-year regime Athens reached peak of power and accomplishment.*
AESCHYLUS (525-456 B.C.)—*Originator of Greek tragedy.*
PHIDIAS (c. 500-432 B.C.)—*Sculptor whose work adorned Parthenon.*
HERODOTUS (c. 484-425 B.C.)—*Father of history.*
SOCRATES (c. 470-399 B.C.)—*Philosopher whose refusal to compromise with truth led to his death.*
PLATO (c. 427-347 B.C.)—*Pupil and biographer of Socrates. His philosophy of the good, the beautiful and the true is set forth in the* Dialogues.
ARISTOTLE (384-322 B.C.)—*Pupil of Plato and tutor of Alexander the Great. Established logic and the scientific method of observation and inductive reasoning, upon which Western thought has been based ever since.*
HIPPOCRATES (c. 460-377 B.C.)—*Father of medicine, whose oath is still recited by graduating physicians.*
EUCLID (c. 300 B.C.)—*Evolved system of geometry.*
ALEXANDER THE GREAT (356-323 B.C.)—*Macedonian king who controlled most of Greece and whose empire spread Greek influence as far as India.*
PLUTARCH (c. 46-120 A.D.)—*Father of biography whose* Parallel Lives *is chief source of information about ancient Greeks and Romans.*
ST. JOHN CHRYSOSTOM (c. 345-407 A.D.)—*Greek church father, Bishop of Constantinople. Stressed asceticism in religion, and knowledge of the Scriptures.*
KING OTTO I (1815-1867)—*Bavarian prince who became first king of Greece, 1832-1862, and was deposed by revolution.*

ELEUTHERIOS VENIZELOS (1864-1936)—*Prime Minister from 1910 to 1935 with few interruptions. He played a significant role in Greece's entry into World War I on Allied side, winning great advantages for postwar Greece. Major figure in the twentieth-century politics and diplomacy of his country.*
NIKOS KAZANTZAKIS (1883-1957)—*Novelist and poet whose heroic sequel to Homer's* Odyssey *has won plaudits.*
DIMITRI MITROPOULOS (1896-1960)—*One of the great musical conductors of the twentieth century.*
KING PAUL I (1901-1964)—*Came to throne in 1947. He and Queen Frederika saw Greece through the difficult years of the Communist rebellion and its return to more normal times.*
KING CONSTANTINE (1941- )—*Son of King Paul I and Queen Frederika. Came to throne in 1964. At twenty-three became the youngest reigning monarch in Europe.*

## SOME IMPORTANT DATES IN GREEK HISTORY

| | |
|---|---|
| c. 1200 B.C. | *Trojan War. Mycenaean army besieges Troy, a city near the Dardanelles.* |
| c. 1100-800 B.C. | *Invasion of Greece by northern tribes that speak a common tongue, basis of Greek language.* |
| 652-510 B.C. | *Hellenic Period. Social reforms are made in Athens, under Solon, but the tyrants—unconstitutional monarchs—rule the city-states of Greece.* |
| 499-478 B.C. | *Persian Wars. After three invasions of Greece by Persian forces, Athens emerges victorious and Greek independence is assured.* |
| 461-429 B.C. | *Athens, under leadership of Pericles, achieves her golden age. Parthenon is begun in 447 B.C.* |
| 431-404 B.C. | *Peloponnesian Wars. Sparta defeats Athens in fight for commercial supremacy. Oligarchy of Thirty Tyrants replaces Athenian democracy.* |
| 338-323 B.C. | *Most of Greece becomes part of Macedonian Empire under Philip and Alexander the Great.* |
| 146 B.C.-330 A.D. | *Greco-Roman Period. Rome rules Greece, but Greek art and culture dominate Rome.* |
| 330-1204 | *Rome falls to northern barbarians. Byzantium, renamed Constantinople, is new capital of Eastern Roman Empire (Byzantine Empire).* |
| 1204-1453 | *Franks and Venetians rule Greece until Turkish conquest.* |
| 1453-1821 | *As part of Ottoman Empire, Greece lies dormant under Turkish rule.* |
| 1821-1829 | *Greek war of independence. Treaty of Adrianople accepted by Turkish Sultan in 1829.* |
| 1832 | *Greece declared an independent kingdom with Prince Otto of Bavaria as king.* |
| 1863 | *George I, a Danish prince, succeeds Otto, establishing the dynasty which has ruled, with some interruptions, to the present day.* |
| 1917-1919 | *Greece enters World War I on side of Allies.* |
| 1924 | *King George II is exiled and the Republic established.* |
| 1935 | *Monarchy is restored after years of political strife.* |
| 1940-1945 | *World War II. After gallant victory over Italian forces, Greece is occupied by German troops.* |
| 1947 | *King Paul succeeds to throne. Communist rebellion is put down in 1949.* |

## SOME GREEK WORDS AND PHRASES

Here is a list of words and phrases you might be likely to use when traveling in Greece. The words are written in simple phonetics for the Greek pronunciation, with the accented syllable in small capitals.

| | |
|---|---|
| Do you speak English? | *mee*-LAH-*tay ah* GLEE-*kah* |
| What do you want? | *tee*-THEH-*leh-teh* |
| How do you say . . . ? | *pohs* LEH-*gheh-teh* |
| Where is (are) . . . ? | *poo* EE-*neh* |
| How far? | POH-*soh mah-kree*-AH |
| Come here. | *eh*-LAH *eh*-THOUGH |
| Please. | *pah-rah-kah*-LOH |
| Pardon. | *seeg*-NOH-*mee* |
| Thank you. | *ehf-kah-rees*-TOH |
| Hello. Goodbye. | YAH-*sass* *Ah*-DEE-*oh* |
| Water | *neh*-ROH |
| Breakfast | PRO-*yev-mah* |
| Dinner | YEV-*mah* |
| Men's room | *ahn*-DROHN |
| Ladies' room | *yee-nee*-KOHN |
| Boat | PLEE-*oh* |
| Automobile (Taxi) | *ahf-toh*-KEE-*nee-toh* |
| Streetcar | *trahm* |
| Bus | *leh-oh-foh*-REE-*oh* |
| Airplane | *ah-eh-roh*-PLAH-*noh* |
| Baggage | *vah*-LEE-*tsess* |
| Hotel | *ksen-oh-toh* KEE-*oh* |

**NUMBERS**

| | |
|---|---|
| One | EH-*nah* |
| Two | DEE-*oh* |
| Three | TREE-*ah* |
| Four | TEH-*seh-rah* |
| Five | PEN-*deh* |
| Six | EK-*see* |
| Seven | *ef*-TAH |
| Eight | *ohk*-TOH |
| Nine | *eh*-NEH-*ah* |
| Ten | DEH-*kah* |
| One hundred | *eh-kah*-TOH |
| One thousand | KEE-*leh-eh* |

**DAYS OF THE WEEK**

| | |
|---|---|
| Sunday | *keer-yah*-KEE |
| Monday | *def*-TEH-*rah* |
| Tuesday | TREE-*tee* |
| Wednesday | *teh*-TAHR-*tee* |
| Thursday | PEMP-*tee* |
| Friday | *pah-rah-skeh*-VEE |
| Saturday | SAH-*vah-toh* |
| Day | *ee*-MEH-*rah* |
| Week | *ev-thoh*-MAH-*thah* |
| Month | MEE-*nahss* |
| Year | KROH-*noss* |
| Today | SEE-*mah-rah* |
| Yesterday | *kthess* |
| Tomorrow | AHV-*ree-oh* |

**MONEY**

| | |
|---|---|
| Drachma | *drak*-MEE |
| Pendara | *pen*-DAH-*rah* |
| Lepta | *lep*-TAH |

## INDEX